NICARAGUA 2016 HUMAN RIGHTS REPORT

EXECUTIVE SUMMARY

Nicaragua is a multiparty constitutional republic, but actions by the ruling Sandinista National Liberation Front (FSLN) party resulted in de facto concentration of power in a single party, with an authoritarian executive branch exercising significant control over the legislative, judicial, and electoral functions. The Supreme Electoral Council (CSE) announced in November the re-election of President Daniel Ortega Saavedra of the FSLN following an electoral process regarded as deeply flawed by domestic organizations and the international community. The elections also expanded the ruling party's supermajority in the National Assembly, which previously allowed for changes in the constitution that extended the reach of executive branch power and the elimination of restrictions on re-election for executive branch officials and mayors. Observers noted serious flaws during the 2012 municipal elections and 2014 regional elections.

Civilian authorities at times did not maintain effective control over the security forces.

The principal human rights abuses were restrictions on citizens' right to vote, biased policies to realize single-party dominance, and increased government harassment and intimidation of nongovernmental organizations (NGOs) and civil society organizations.

Additional significant human rights abuses included arbitrary police arrest and detention of suspects, including abuse during detention; harsh and life-threatening prison conditions with arbitrary and lengthy pretrial detention; obstacles to freedom of speech and press, including government intimidation and harassment of journalists and independent media, as well as increased restriction of access to public information, including national statistics from public offices. There was also widespread corruption, including in the police, CSE, Supreme Court of Justice (CSJ), and other government organs; societal violence, particularly against women and lesbian, gay, bisexual, transgender, and intersex (LGBTI) persons; trafficking in persons; discrimination against ethnic minorities and indigenous persons and communities; societal discrimination against persons with disabilities; discrimination against persons with HIV/AIDS; and violations of trade union rights.

The government rarely took steps to prosecute officials who committed abuses, whether in the security services or elsewhere in government. Impunity remained a widespread problem.

Section 1. Respect for the Integrity of the Person, Including Freedom from:

a. Arbitrary Deprivation of Life and other Unlawful or Politically Motivated Killings

There were several reports the government or its agents committed arbitrary or unlawful killings, many during confrontations with illegal armed groups in the northern part of the country; however, a lack of clear and impartial investigations into deaths made attribution difficult. Human rights organizations and independent media alleged some killings were politically motivated.

On April 18, Andres Cerrato was kidnapped, shot, and killed in the community of San Martin de Daca, in Ayapal, Jinotega. As early as February, Cerrato reportedly experienced repeated harassment by the Nicaraguan National Police (NNP) and army, which accused him of aiding politically motivated armed groups in the region. Cerrato's family claimed armed men forcibly took him from his home at or after midnight. His body was found approximately three miles from his home later that day, bearing gunshot wounds and signs of torture. Prior to his death, Cerrato had claimed that soldiers entered his home in March and forcibly coerced him into confessing to having information on members of armed groups, although Cerrato denied any ties to the groups. Following Cerrato's death, the army stated it did not conduct such operations and did not have information on the case.

Reports of shootings were increasingly common in the area of Jinotega. These shootings were widely believed to be related to the army's pursuit of what many refer to as armed antigovernment groups in the north central region, although the army claims only the presence of criminals and/or delinquents.

There were no developments in or investigations of the January 2015 killing of Modesto Duarte Altamirano or the 2014 killing of Carlos Garcia, a former Contra and member of the Independent Liberal Party (see also section 1.d., "Role of the Police and Security Apparatus").

b. Disappearance

There were no reports of politically motivated disappearances.

c. Torture and Other Cruel, Inhuman, or Degrading Treatment or Punishment

Although the law prohibits such practices, there were numerous reports that police abused suspects during arrest, used excessive force, and engaged in degrading treatment. In the first six months of the year, the NGO Nicaraguan Human Rights Center (CENIDH) received 610 complaints against the NNP for excessive force, arbitrary detention, and cruel or degrading treatment, including in prisons. CENIDH was able to confirm abuse in 391 of those complaints.

There were numerous claims of torture by agents of the Directorate of Judicial Assistance (DAJ), a special police investigations unit, especially during arrests related to organized crime. Human rights organizations alleged the directorate operated outside the normal NNP chain of authority and was not accountable to normal NNP internal affairs procedures.

Following their release, two prisoners arrested for involvement in a 2014 attack on an FSLN bus caravan claimed to the press that they were regularly beaten while in the DAJ prison. Additionally, a Mexican student reportedly held in custody at the DAJ prison for nine days appeared for his trial with bloodshot eyes and bruises. Prison officials claimed that the bruising was "self-inflicted" to discredit the government.

Prison and Detention Center Conditions

Prison conditions were harsh and potentially life threatening. Overcrowding, poor sanitation, difficulties obtaining medical care, and violence among prisoners remained serious problems in prison facilities.

<u>Physical Conditions</u>: Overcrowding remained a problem. Pretrial detainees often shared cells with convicted prisoners. Juvenile prisoners shared cells with adults due to overcrowding. Human rights organizations reported police regularly left suspects in holding cells during their trials due to negligence or a lack of funds to transport them to court.

Prison conditions continued to deteriorate due to antiquated infrastructure and increasing inmate populations. Many prisoners suffered mistreatment from prison officials and other inmates. Inmates also suffered from parasites, inadequate medical attention, frequent food shortages, contaminated water, and inadequate sanitation. Released prisoners and family members of prisoners reported there was poor ventilation and lighting in the DAJ prison. Family members, churches, and charitable organizations supplemented the national budget of 10 cordobas ($0.35) per prisoner per day for food. There was no budget allocation for health or personal care.

Conditions for female inmates were generally better than those for men but were nevertheless overcrowded and unhygienic.

Conditions in jails and temporary holding cells were also harsh. Most facilities were physically decrepit and infested with vermin; had inadequate ventilation, electricity, or sewage systems; and lacked potable water.

Administration: Recordkeeping on prisoners was inadequate, and the government took no steps to improve it. The problem was particularly serious in the North Caribbean Autonomous Region (RACN) and the South Caribbean Autonomous Region (RACS). In certain instances, the government restricted prisoners' access to visitors, attorneys, physicians, and human rights officials. Although prisoners and detainees could submit complaints to judicial authorities without censorship and request investigation of credible allegations of inhuman conditions, authorities often ignored or did not process complaints. The extent to which the government investigated allegations of poor prison conditions was unknown. The government ombudsman could serve on behalf of prisoners and detainees to consider such matters as informal alternatives to incarceration for nonviolent offenders, although this generally did not occur. The government announced in February that it had provided early release to more than 8,000 prisoners since 2014, and in November it further stated that approximately 1,600 additional prisoners serving less than five years for misdemeanors had been released on parole. Due to a lack of consistent national statistics from previous years, it was difficult to estimate the impact of these releases on prison conditions.

Independent Monitoring: The government frequently denied prison visits by local human rights groups as well as the media. The government denied CENIDH access to all prison facilities when it attempted to investigate reports of hazardous conditions. NGOs generally received complaints through family members of inmates and often were unable to follow up on cases until after the release of the prisoner, due to lack of access.

d. Arbitrary Arrest or Detention

The law prohibits arbitrary arrest and detention, but the government and its agents did not always comply with or enforce the law. Human rights NGOs noted several cases of arbitrary arrests by the NNP and army, including irregular arrests and detentions while the NNP investigated armed opposition groups in the Pacific north of the country.

Role of the Police and Security Apparatus

The constitution establishes the NNP as an apolitical, nonpartisan institution protecting all citizens equally under the law. The NNP Office of Internal Affairs is responsible for investigating complaints and abuses regarding police officers or internal police activities. Many duties previously held by the Ministry of Interior to administer the NNP, with the president as commander in chief, were transferred to the presidency in accordance with changes made to the constitution in 2014. The Ministry of Interior and the NNP each have law enforcement and internal security responsibilities throughout the country. The Ministry of Interior oversees the General Directorate for Migration and Foreigner Services, which works together with the police to oversee topics of migration and border security.

The army is responsible for external security but also has some domestic responsibilities, including countering illicit trafficking in narcotics and providing for the transportation of election-related materials, including ballots. Many informed observers in civil society and the independent press regarded the army functionally as an autonomous force responding directly to the president, following a series of constitutional and military code reforms enacted in 2014, which gave the president greater control over the armed forces. The Office of the Inspectorate General is responsible for investigating abuses and corruption in the army, but limited public information was available on its activities.

There were instances in which the government failed to maintain effective control over the NNP, and the government failed to investigate and punish abuse and corruption. There continued to be numerous reports of impunity involving security forces.

The NNP Office of Internal Affairs, and to a lesser extent the Office of the Inspector General, are responsible for investigating police abuse; however, corruption, inefficiency, and lack of transparency of the justice system contributed to a public perception of police impunity. According to a report by the Inter-American Commission on Human Rights, in 2015 the NNP received 162 complaints of use of excessive force. Of these, the NNP investigated 127 and found officers guilty in 93. Information on the final disposition of those found guilty was not available. Due to the lack of specificity on the activities of the Office of Internal Affairs and a general lack of access to government information, human rights organizations and experts on security found it difficult to assess how the NNP investigated allegations of human rights violations by its members. The government generally did not take action on complaints against security forces.

NGOs reported that President Ortega had politicized the NNP and led many to question its professionalism. For instance, the president renewed the tenure of the national chief of police for a third consecutive term, making her the longest standing police chief since 1990. The extension was legal under changes to the constitution in 2014, but the president had previously extended her term through a 2011 executive decree that allegedly violated term limits prescribed in law at the time. The extension followed after sweeping changes to the police code granted the president greater power over the NNP. The media also highlighted the NNP's use of an emblem with President Ortega and Sandino's shadow as part of the officer's uniform, and the use of the FSLN red and black party flag painted on select police stations or at police celebrations. NGOs and the press alleged the NNP continued to provide preferential treatment for progovernment and FSLN rallies.

The 2015 Sovereign Security Law significantly broadened the definition of state sovereignty and security and established a National Committee of Sovereign Security (NCSS), an executive-level committee with the enforcement backing of the military. The law defines "sovereign security" as the "existence of permanent peace" within the country and states the government is responsible to protect against "any risk, threat, or conflict that puts itself against sovereign security." The law includes "any other factor that creates danger to the security of the people, life, family, and community, as well as the supreme interests of the Nicaraguan nation," when outlining potential risks and threats to the nation's sovereign security. The law stipulates the NCSS, made up of representatives from the NNP and the military, has the power to dispatch security forces. Human rights groups continued to express strong concern over the law and its implications on democratic space in the country.

Impunity remained a problem. There were no developments in the 2013 killing of four civilians, including former Contra leader Joaquin Torres Diaz, alias "Cascabel," or the 2013 killing of Yairon Diaz Pastrana in Pantasma, all allegedly killed by military forces. According to local NGOs, there was no effort to investigate police beatings of and use of excessive force against demonstrators during 2013 protests in front of the Nicaraguan Social Security Institute. The NNP and prosecutors declared they had no official evidence of the event to continue an investigation, despite videos on YouTube and other public media.

Likewise, there were no developments in the 2012 death of former Contra Santos Guadalupe Joyas Borge ("Pablo Negro") or in the 2012 case of community leaders Pedro Ramon Castro and Miguel Angel Oliva, who allegedly were killed by four NNP members in the municipality of Pantasma.

Arrest Procedures and Treatment of Detainees

The law requires police to obtain a warrant from a judicial authority prior to detaining a suspect and to notify family members of the detainee's whereabouts within 24 hours. While the law also stipulates a prosecutor accompany police making an arrest, CENIDH claimed irregularities in arrest procedures led to arbitrary arrest and detentions.

Police may hold a suspect legally for 48 hours before arraignment, when they must bring the person before a judge. A judge then must order the suspect released or transferred to jail for pretrial detention. After the initial 48 hours, the suspect should be allowed family member visits. The detainee has the right to bail unless a judge deems there is a flight risk. In most instances detainees were informed of charges against them, although there were instances when this did not occur, and at other times there were delays. Detainees have the right to an attorney immediately following their arrest, and the state provides indigent detainees with a public defender.

Arbitrary Arrest: According to NGOs and other human rights groups, arbitrary arrests occurred regularly. There were numerous reports of the use of the DAJ jail cells for arbitrary arrests for more than the prescribed 48 hours of detention legally allowed. Many arrests were allegedly made without warrants and without informing family members or legal counsel.

Pretrial Detention: Lengthy pretrial detention continued to be a problem, especially in the RACN and the RACS, where detainees often waited an average of six months for their cases to be presented to a judge. Observers attributed delays to limited facilities, an overburdened judicial system, judicial inaction, and high crime rates. No information was available on the percentage of the prison population in pretrial detention or the national average length of pretrial detention.

<u>Detainee's Ability to Challenge Lawfulness of Detention before a Court</u>: While the law provides detainees the ability to challenge the legality of their detention before a court, procedural information for doing so was not publically available. There were reports on the obstacles legal counsels faced when they attempted to invoke constitutional protections for detainees, including habeas corpus, and courts frequently ignored their requests.

e. Denial of Fair Public Trial

Although the law provides for an independent judiciary, the judicial system did not function independently. The law requires vetting of new judicial appointments by the CSJ, a process unduly affected by nepotism, personal influence, and political affiliation. Once appointed, many judges submitted to political and economic pressures that compromised their independence. NGOs complained of a delay of justice caused by judicial inaction and widespread impunity, especially regarding family and domestic violence and sexual abuse. Authorities occasionally failed to respect court orders.

Trial Procedures

The constitution provides for the right to a fair public trial, but the judiciary did not always enforce this right. Defendants are presumed innocent until proven guilty. Defendants have the right to be fully informed of the charges against them and the right to a fair trial. While the law establishes specific time periods for cases to come to trial, most cases encountered undue delay. Trials are public, but in some cases involving minors or at the victim's request, they may be private. The law requires that defendants must be present at their trial, although this was not always respected. Defendants have the right to legal counsel, and the state provides public defenders for indigent persons. Defendants have the right to adequate time and facilities to prepare a defense and access to all information and evidence registered with the government, as well as the right to know why and how it was obtained, but only during the discovery and trial phases, not during the pretrial period. Although the constitution recognizes indigenous languages, defendants were not granted court translators. Defendants may confront and question witnesses and have the right to appeal a conviction. Defendants may present their own witnesses and evidence in their defense; however, some judges refused to admit evidence on behalf of the defense. Defendants cannot be compelled to testify or confess guilt. The law extends these rights to all citizens regardless of gender, ethnicity, disability, or other status.

Independent press reported the court system had unofficial orders to forego jail time or pretrial detention in domestic violence cases. The president of the CSJ did not refute these claims but instead reinforced that judges were free to act independently in these matters, while also referring to issues of overcrowding in prisons and preventive detention facilities. According to reports, this order applied only to domestic violence cases considered mild.

Political Prisoners and Detainees

There was no reliable information available on the number or treatment of political prisoners.

Civil Judicial Procedures and Remedies

Individuals and organizations may file suit in civil courts to seek damages for human rights violations, but authorities did not always respect court orders.

The lack of an effective civil law system resulted in some civil matters being pursued as criminal cases because criminal cases were often resolved more quickly. In a number of instances, individuals and groups appealed to the Inter-American Commission of Human Rights (IACHR), which passed their cases to the Inter-American Court of Human Rights.

Property Restitution

While the government resolved some property claims during the year, it regularly failed to enforce court orders with respect to seizure, restitution, or compensation of private property. Enforcement of court orders was frequently subject to nonjudicial considerations. Members of the judiciary, including those at senior levels, were widely believed to be corrupt or subject to political pressure. The government failed to evict those who illegally took possession of private property.

Several foreign citizens claimed they were arrested and at times sentenced for unrelated--and they claimed untrue--crimes, due to outstanding property disputes with well-placed citizens of the country. In April, Juan Venerio Espinales was found guilty of shooting and killing two men who were part of a group of squatters allegedly attempting to seize his property in Chinandega. He stated that he did so only after authorities failed to take action in the matter.

The Small Business Enterprise Association, several domestic NGOs, and opposition members alleged the government seized minor private property such as laptops, cell phones, and vehicles without due process.

f. Arbitrary or Unlawful Interference with Privacy, Family, Home, or Correspondence

While the law prohibits such actions, several domestic NGOs, members of the Catholic Church, and opposition members alleged the government monitored their e-mail and telephone conversations.

Inhabitants in northern towns, particularly in the departments of Nueva Segovia, Jinotega, and Madriz, as well as the RACS and the RACN, alleged repeated government interrogations and searches without cause or warrant, related to supposed support for armed groups, while government officials claimed they were confronting common criminals.

The ruling party reportedly required citizens to demonstrate party membership in order to obtain or retain employment in the public sector and have access to public social programs.

Section 2. Respect for Civil Liberties, Including:

a. Freedom of Speech and Press

The constitution provides for freedom of speech and press, but the government used administrative, judicial, and financial means to limit the exercise of these rights. Although the law provides that the right to information cannot be subjected to censorship, it also establishes retroactive liability, including criminal penalties for libel and slander.

Freedom of Speech and Expression: Some individuals suffered reprisals for expressing opinions in public on matters of special importance to the ruling party. On February 26, civil society figure Carlos Bonilla and his wife and fellow activist, Gabriela Garcia, both well-known members of the opposition and outspoken critics of the government, received multiple knife wounds and bruises when five men attacked them. The two were on their way to present the CSE with results from a survey conducted by their organization regarding public perception of inefficiency and corruption within the CSE. According to eyewitness reports, neighbors captured and held two of the attackers and presented them to the police. The police never announced an investigation into the attack and never released any information on the whereabouts of the detained.

<u>Press and Media Freedoms</u>: Independent media faced official and unofficial restrictions, reprisals, and harassment but were generally allowed to express a variety of views. The government restricted media freedom through harassment, censorship, and use of arbitrary justifications based on pending legislation and alleged national security concerns. Private individuals sympathetic to the government also harassed the media for criticizing the government.

On October 7, Carlos Fernando Chamorro, a prominent civil society leader and owner of the leading investigative weekly newspaper *Confidencial*, said that in September, two workers on his staff were separately approached and intimidated by members of the ruling party and by a military official. In each case the party members questioned the staffers on the internal workings of the newspaper, requested a list of visitors to the offices, access codes to the newspaper website, and descriptions of the security measures protecting their workplace. The military dismissed Chamorro's accusations.

The government continued to use direct and indirect means to pressure and seek to close independent media outlets, allegedly for political reasons. Independent media owners continued to express concern that incidents of vandalism, seizure of broadcast equipment, and fear of criminal defamation charges created a climate of self-censorship, which the government could exploit to limit press freedom. Independent news outlets reported that generally they were not permitted to attend official government events, were denied interviews by government officials, and received restricted or no direct access to government information. Official media, however, were not similarly restricted.

Since 2008 the General Law (Law 200) on Telecommunications has been in review in the National Assembly. Until the reforms are approved or denied, media outlets are unable to apply for new broadcasting licenses. Nevertheless, the government granted licenses in a discretionary manner and extended the validity of existing licenses indefinitely. Human rights groups and the media criticized the legal insecurity created by the lack of telecommunications legislation, given that Law 200 regulates routine administrative processes, such as the purchase and import of goods related to broadcasting and license adjudication. Furthermore, radio owners reported were afraid of deferring long-term investments due to the lack of updated licenses.

In one example, the transfer of ownership of leading independent radio station Radio Dario in Leon, following the 2014 death of the station's founder, Juan Toruno, remained unresolved. Toruno's son, who served as Radio Dario's general manager, filed documents shortly after his father's death for the administrative action of transferring ownership. Citing the pending status of Law 200, officials had yet to finalize the process, leaving the station vulnerable to seizure or closure.

The Communications Research Center of Nicaragua (CINCO) reported that control over television media by the FSLN and President Ortega continued throughout the year. National television increasingly was controlled either by business associates of the president or directly owned and administered by President Ortega's family members. Eight of the 10 basic channels available were under direct FSLN influence or owned and controlled by persons with close ties to the government.

Generally, media stations owned by the presidential family limited news programming and served as outlets for progovernment or FSLN propaganda and campaign advertisements. Press and human rights organizations claimed the use of state funds for official media, as well as biased distribution of government advertising dollars, placed independent outlets at an unfair disadvantage. Independent media asserted the moratorium on granting new government broadcasting licenses, combined with the uncertainties of the National Assembly's protracted telecommunications review, contributed to legal insecurity and shrinking opportunities for private investment. Some independent media owners also alleged the government exerted pressure on private firms to limit their advertising in the independent media, although other observers believed the lack of advertising was the result of self-censorship by private companies or a business decision based on circulation numbers.

In January officials, apparently from the Nicaraguan Telecommunications Office, seized the broadcast equipment of independent station Radio Emperador. The individuals overseeing the seizure were not identifiable as public servants and did not present themselves as such, yet they informed officials from the station that the station's documentation was not in order.

<u>Violence and Harassment</u>: One of the largest daily newspapers, opposition-leaning *La Prensa*, claimed that government officials and supporters regularly intimidated journalists, actively hindered investigations, and failed to respond to questions on a variety of problems, particularly those involving the constitution, rule of law, and corruption. There were several reported cases of threats against the press.

<u>Censorship or Content Restrictions</u>: Many journalists practiced self-censorship, fearing economic and physical repercussions for investigative reporting on crime or official corruption. Additionally, media outlet owners exercised self-censorship by choosing not to publish news that affected public perceptions of the government or the FSLN. Slander and libel are both punishable under the law with fines structured around the minimum wage. The penalties for slander and libel range from 120 to 300 times the minimum daily wage.

The government continued to enforce the controversial Law 528, or "Ley Arce," which print media owners and international NGOs claimed restricted the public's access to independent and opposition newspapers through the establishment of high tariffs and bureaucratic delays on the importation of ink, paper, machinery, and other printing necessities, despite protections in the constitution protecting the right to freedom from tariffs for media. Journalist organizations expressed concern regarding the lack of government support for the media sector and their organizations.

<u>Libel/Slander Laws</u>: Although during the year the government did not use libel laws or cite national security to suppress publications, independent media reported engaging in self-censorship due to the government's previous use of libel laws.

Internet Freedom

The government did not restrict or disrupt access to the internet or censor online content; however, several NGOs claimed the government monitored their e-mail without appropriate legal authority. Additionally, paid government supporters used social media and website commentary spaces to harass prominent members of civil society, human rights defenders, and a well-known journalist.

The International Telecommunication Union reported that approximately 20 percent of citizens used the internet in 2015.

Academic Freedom and Cultural Events

There were some government restrictions on academic freedom, and many academics and researchers reported pressure to censor themselves. There were no government restrictions on cultural events.

Human rights NGOs and civil society groups reported authorities required students in elementary and secondary public schools to participate in progovernment rallies while schools were in session. Political propaganda for the ruling party was seen on walls inside public schools. Teacher organizations and NGOs alleged continuing FSLN interference in the school system through the use of school facilities as FSLN campaign headquarters, favoritism shown to members of FSLN youth groups or children of FSLN members, politicized issuance of scholarships, and the use of pro-FSLN education materials.

b. Freedom of Peaceful Assembly and Association

Freedom of Assembly

The law recognizes the right to public assembly, demonstration, and mobilization but requires demonstrators to obtain permission for a rally or march by registering its planned size and location with the police. CENIDH and the Permanent Commission for Human Rights (CPDH) reported police generally protected or otherwise gave preferential treatment to progovernment FSLN demonstrations while disrupting or denying registration for opposition groups. In many cases police did not protect opposition protesters when progovernment supporters harassed or attacked them.

On November 30, groups opposing the planned construction of an interoceanic canal organized a nationwide protest centered in Managua. Organizers reported that police arbitrarily stopped thousands of protesters and prevented their participation, using tactics that included a heavy deployment of antiriot police at key rural intersections leading to the capital, using heavy machinery to block bridges and roads near communities where protesters lived and threatening to revoke licenses or seize buses and trucks from companies transporting demonstrators. NNP officials seized two vehicles owned by protest organizer and recognized leader of the anti-canal movement, Francisca Ramirez. The vehicles were later returned with significant damage. The NNP reportedly used rubber bullets on protesters, injuring several, and there were reports of traffic backups of up to 12 miles on highways leading into the capital due to checkpoints.

Freedom of Association

The law provides for freedom of association, including the right to organize or affiliate with political parties; however, the CSE and National Assembly used their accreditation powers for political purposes. National Assembly accreditation is mandatory for NGOs to receive donations. Domestic NGOs complained the

Ortega administration's control of access to funding from foreign donors reduced their ability to operate.

c. Freedom of Religion

See the Department of State's *International Religious Freedom Report* at www.state.gov/religiousfreedomreport/.

d. Freedom of Movement, Internally Displaced Persons, Protection of Refugees, and Stateless Persons

The law provides for freedom of internal movement, foreign travel, emigration, and repatriation for citizens and the government generally respected these rights. The government strictly controlled the entry of persons affiliated with some groups, specifically humanitarian and faith-based organizations.

Abuse of Migrants, Refugees, and Stateless Persons: The government enforced strict controls for migrants seeking to cross the country from Costa Rica. The government reported the drowning deaths of at least 10 illegal migrants in Lake Nicaragua.

The Nicaraguan National Commission for Refugees had not met since 2015. The Office of the UN High Commissioner for Refugees (UNHCR) noted that migration authorities generally refused to register any new asylum applications. UNHCR reported that in 2015, 185 new applications for asylum were registered but had not yet been considered. Another 205 claims were reported during the year, but UNHCR did not have further information on government actions regarding these requests. Opposition members noted the contrast between a lack of response to new requests for refugee status and asylum by the government, and the promptness with which former Salvadorian President Mauricio Funes received political asylum status. Without access to official information, it was impossible to know of other requests that were accepted and the swiftness with which they were processed.

Protection of Refugees

Access to Asylum: The law provides for the granting of asylum or refugee status, and the government has established a system for providing protection to refugees. Only the executive branch or the country's embassies abroad may grant asylum for political persecution.

<u>Durable Solutions</u>: According to UNHCR, the government recognized 61 persons for refugee status in 2015.

Section 3. Freedom to Participate in the Political Process

The law provides citizens the ability to choose their government in free and fair periodic elections based on universal and equal suffrage and conducted by secret ballot; however, the government in previous years restricted the exercise of this ability and took further measures to do so during the reporting year.

January 2014 constitutional reforms allow uniformed military and police officials to hold public office, allow indefinite re-election, and extend the terms of public officers indefinitely if the National Assembly does not name new officers.

The November 6 elections for president, vice president, national assembly members, and representatives for the Central American parliament did not meet the conditions of being free and fair. Domestic observers, business leaders, representatives of the Catholic Church, and many members of society believed that with the lack of accredited national and international observers, the control of the ruling party over most of the societal checks to prove the fairness of the elections, and the ruling party's use of its control over other branches of government to halt the participation of any significant opposition resulted in an illegitimate electoral process.

Elections and Political Participation

<u>Recent Elections</u>: The November 6 presidential and legislative elections were marred by allegations of institutional fraud and the absence of independent opposition political parties. National observers and opposition leaders claimed rates of abstention from 60 to 70 percent, contrary to the 68.2 percent voter participation rate posted by the CSE. Opposition party members also reported that government officials transported supporters of the ruling party to voting centers. Opposition party members and observers claimed the ruling party used its control over the CSE to commit fraud. There were reports of public-sector employees being pressured to vote and show proof the next day at work that they had voted. National observers and opposition representatives claimed that opposition poll watchers were denied accreditation, FSLN-affiliated poll watchers posed as opposition poll workers, and votes were not counted in accordance with the law.

<u>Political Parties and Political Participation</u>: The FSLN used state resources for political activities to enhance its electoral advantage in recent elections. The FSLN made party membership mandatory for an increasing number of public sector employees. The CPDH and the Nicaraguan Pro Human Rights Association (ANPDH) reported that employees in various state institutions were required to affiliate with the FSLN, and that to apply for a government position an applicant must receive a written recommendation from the FSLN. The ANPDH also received reports the FSLN automatically deducted party dues from the paychecks of certain state employees.

The FSLN also used its authority to decide who could obtain national identity cards (cedulas). Persons without identity cards had difficulty participating in the legal economy, conducting bank transactions, or voting. Such persons also were subject to restrictions in employment, access to courts, and land ownership. Civil society organizations continued to express concern about the politicized distribution of identity cards, alleging this was how the FSLN attempted to manipulate past elections and that the CSE failed to provide identity cards to opposition members while widely distributing them to party loyalists.

On June 8, the CSJ issued a ruling five years after the filing of a suit over the legal representation of the opposition Independent Liberal Party (PLI). The CSJ ruled against the PLI's representative and main opposition coordinator, Eduardo Montealegre, transferring the party to a legal representative widely considered beholden to the FSLN, Pedro Reyes.

As the party receiving the second most votes in the 2011 presidential election, the PLI was constitutionally entitled to designate party representatives to sit on Municipal Electoral Councils (CEMs) and Departmental Electoral Councils (CEDs) along with representatives of the FSLN. The CEMs and CEDs resolve electoral disputes and provide oversight of the electoral process by geographic regions. The timing of the CSJ ruling severely curtailed the PLI's ability to fill these positions, allowing the FSLN to fill these bodies with its supporters. Observers also noted that these actions, in conjunction with President Ortega's June 4 announcement that there would be no national or international observation of the elections, left no mechanism for credible, independent oversight during the November elections.

On July 29, at Pedro Reyes' request, the CSE removed 28 PLI national assembly members from their elected positions because they refused to recognize the new leadership.

On November 18, Pedro Reyes confirmed reports that he had been removed as national president of the PLI, claiming that the CSE informed him that his removal came at the behest of the party's executive board and was in accordance with PLI party rules. Reyes stated the CSE further advised him that he was blocked from participating in party activities for three years.

<u>Participation of Women and Minorities</u>: Constitutional reforms in 2014 mandated equal representation of men and women in all elected bodies, including councilmembers, mayors and vice mayors, and representatives to the National Assembly. Observers viewed these changes as superficial, noting that women in these positions did not hold significant power or influence within their respective bodies. While the law does not mention the presidential and vice presidential positions specifically, all parties but one presented a man and a woman as their presidential and vice presidential candidates, respectively, for the November elections. Some opposition parties expressed fear of being disqualified from the ballot if they did not meet the requirement of equal representation for the presidential ballot, despite this not being an explicit requirement of the law.

Section 4. Corruption and Lack of Transparency in Government

The law provides criminal penalties for official corruption; however, the government did not enforce the law effectively, and officials frequently engaged in corrupt practices with impunity.

Executive branch officials continued to disburse economic and developmental assistance funds lent by the Venezuelan-led Bolivarian Alliance for the Peoples of Our America (ALBA), which averaged more than $550 million dollars per year from 2010 to 2013 but has recently plummeted to approximately $200 million in 2016, outside the normal budgetary process controlled by the legislature. The media reported that ALBA-funded contracts were awarded to companies with ties to the Ortega family and noted the funds from Venezuela served as a separate budget tightly controlled by the FSLN, with little public oversight. Cases of mismanagement of these funds by public officials were reportedly handled personally by members of the ruling party, rather than by the government entities in charge of oversight of public funds.

Independent media, human rights groups, and opposition parties reported President Ortega's administration blurred distinctions between the FSLN and the government through its use of FSLN-led family cabinets (community-based bodies that administer government social programs) and party-controlled Sandinista leadership committees (CLSs). The government administered subsidized food, housing, vaccinations, access to clinics, and other benefits directly through either the family cabinets or CLS system, which reportedly often coerced citizens into FSLN membership and denied services to opposition members. Persons seeking to obtain or retain public sector employment, national identity documents, or voter registration were obliged to obtain recommendation letters from CLS block captains. The government continued to devolve legal responsibilities to family cabinets, specifically regarding mediation processes in cases of domestic violence.

Indigenous leaders, property owners, and civil society organizations continued to request detailed information and express objections to the 2013 100-year concession given to the Hong Kong Nicaraguan Canal Development Investment Company to build and operate an interoceanic canal through the country. A number of organizations, human rights groups, and landowners, collectively known as the National Council for the Defense of our Land, Lake, and National Sovereignty, tried formally to challenge the law that allows the concession in both the National Assembly and the CSJ. Both institutions, however, blocked these requests.

Corruption: Companies reported that bribery of public officials, unlawful seizures, and arbitrary assessments by customs and tax authorities were common. In a survey of 2,500 companies, one-third of all respondents reported arbitrary and illegal actions by government offices that regulate property rights and business establishment.

The courts remained particularly susceptible to bribes, manipulation, and other forms of corruption, especially by the FSLN, giving the sense that the FSLN heavily influenced CSJ and lower-level court actions. In February the press reported on the release of more than 8,000 prisoners since 2014 through a program that existed outside the Ministry of Interior and bypassed the legal judicial process that provides judges sole authorization for prisoner releases. The government confirmed the release and justified it as a program to provide for the humanitarian release of prisoners and reunite families. Human rights organizations, however, noted that several prisoners who had previously received court orders for release, issued through the judicial system, remained incarcerated. Private-sector representatives additionally reported an increase in judicial corruption for extorting money.

<u>Financial Disclosure</u>: Public officials were subject to financial disclosure laws.
The law requires these declarations be made public and provides for sanctions in
cases of noncompliance. In practice few public officers made these declarations
public, and there was no public record of sanctions for noncompliance. The Office
of the Comptroller is responsible for combating corruption within government
agencies and offices. Observers, however, questioned the impartiality of the
comptroller, especially concerning the lack of oversight of ALBA funds given
directly to the government. Since 2007 the comptroller had not investigated any
government office or mandated sanctions due to noncompliance as required by
law.

<u>Public Access to Information</u>: Although the law mandates public access to
government information and statistics, lack of transparency and access to
information remained serious problems. Government budget documents were
widely and easily accessible to the general public, but they did not provide a
complete picture of revenues and expenditures. For example, the government did
not account for the expenditure of significant off-budget assistance from
Venezuela (see above), and this assistance was not subject to audit or legislative
oversight. Delays and denial of information were common, while appeals
mechanisms were overly burdensome and slow. Control of government
information is centralized in the Communication and Citizenship Council, headed
by First Lady Rosario Murillo, but there is no provision for that office in the law.
Media and civil society organizations, such as CINCO and Foundation Violeta
Barrios de Chamorro, repeatedly reported that requests for official information
without express authorization from the council were often refused. The law
provides for exceptions to disclosure in cases related to national security and trade
secrets. There are no mandated timelines for compliance with disclosure requests.

**Section 5. Governmental Attitude Regarding International and
Nongovernmental Investigation of Alleged Violations of Human Rights**

A variety of domestic and international human rights groups operated in the
country. Humanitarian organizations faced obstacles to operating or expulsion,
and government officials harassed and intimidated domestic and international
NGOs that were critical of the government or the FSLN. Some NGOs reported
that intimidation by government officials created a climate of fear intended to
suppress criticism. The government continued to prevent non-FSLN-affiliated
NGOs and civil society groups from participating in government social programs,
such as Programa Amor and Hambre Cero, and it frequently used FSLN-controlled
family cabinets or CLSs to administer these programs. Increased government

restrictions on domestic NGOs' ability to receive funding directly from international donors seriously hindered the NGOs' ability to operate. Additionally, increased control over the admission of foreign visitors or volunteer groups into the country hindered the work of humanitarian groups and human rights NGOs. Some groups reported difficulties in moving donated goods through customs.

Domestic NGOs under government investigation reported problems accessing the justice system and delays in filing petitions, as well as pressure from state authorities. Many NGOs believed comptroller and tax authorities audited their accounts as a means of intimidation. While legally permitted, spot audits were a common form of harassment and often used selectively, according to NGOs. NGOs reported difficulties in scheduling meetings with authorities and in receiving official information due to a growing culture of secrecy. NGOs also reported hostility or aggression when questioning or speaking with officials on subjects such as corruption and the rule of law.

The United Nations or Other International Bodies: In August the UN special rapporteur on the situation of human rights defenders cancelled a planned trip to the country, citing a lack of approval from the UN security office. Local partner organizations stated that they believed there were additional concerns regarding the rapporteur's visit, following the government's expulsions earlier in the year of individuals working on human rights issues. The government did not send a representative to the April hearings of the IACHR, which convened a private meeting at the request of CENIDH to discuss government inaction on precautionary measures provided by IACHR to CENIDH in 2008. Two public hearings regarding general human rights issues also convened, in April and December, in which the government chose not to participate. The IACHR had made the request to visit the country several times in previous sessions and had received a promise from the government to process its request.

In February the government detained, revoked the entry permit for, and expelled Carlos Ponce, Latin America director of Freedom House. Ponce was visiting the country to present the organization's 2015 Freedom in the World Report on Nicaragua. Officials stated that he had attempted to enter on a passport of a different nationality than he had used for previous entries. There were a number of other detentions and expulsions of foreign visitors whose visits focused on matters considered sensitive to the ruling party, such as alleged criticism on human rights, rule of law, and the interoceanic canal.

<u>Government Human Rights Bodies</u>: In April the administration named Corina Centeno as head of the Office of the Ombudsman for Human Rights (PDDH). Human rights organizations responded to her appointment with criticism, noting her prior experience working with health labor unions and her affiliation with the FSLN. The PDDH was perceived as politicized and ineffective.

The National Assembly operated a human rights committee focused primarily on amnesties and pardons. Civil society organizations viewed the committee as deadlocked by partisan political forces and lacking credibility.

Section 6. Discrimination, Societal Abuses, and Trafficking in Persons

Women

<u>Rape and Domestic Violence</u>: The law criminalizes all forms of rape, regardless of the relationship between the victim and the accused. Sentences for those convicted of rape range from eight to 12 years, or 15 years in cases of aggravated rape. The law criminalizes domestic violence and provides prison sentences ranging from one to 12 years. The government failed to enforce the law effectively, leading to widespread impunity and reports of increased violence from released offenders emboldened by their release. Many women were reluctant to report abuse due to enforced medical examinations for survivors of rape and other sexual crimes, social stigma, fear of retribution, impunity for perpetrators, and loss of economic security if abusive spouses were jailed. While the law provides for the issuance of restraining orders, problems in their effective enforcement continued. Observers reported a general increase in sexual crimes against women compared with 2015. The NNP reported 1,458 cases of rape and aggravated rape and 862 cases of sexual abuse in 2015, the most recent data available. The Institute of Legal Medicine within the judicial branch, however, reported investigating 5,596 incidents of sexual violence in 2015, constituting more than 7 percent of their investigations. There were no comprehensive statistics available on prosecutions or convictions. Human rights organizations and women's rights groups alleged that many of the early releases of recent years (see section 1.c.) were of men who had been convicted of attacking women, but these claims could not be verified.

Violence against women remained high, according to domestic NGO reports. The NGO Catholics for the Right to Decide reported that between January and July, 41 women were killed, many of whom were raped, beaten, or maimed. NGOs working on women's issues reported an increase in the severity of these crimes over the past seven years. Women's rights organizations claimed police generally understated the level of violence against women. For example, in 2015 the NNP recognized 16 femicides, while the NGO Network of Women Against Violence reported 53 that year. Women's rights NGOs continued to protest the presidential decree on regulations for the Comprehensive Law (Law 779) on Violence Against Women, which encompasses the legal protections for women against violence, because it dilutes protections found in the law.

NNP commissariats were established in 1993 as independent offices designed to provide social and legal help to women, mediate spousal conflicts, investigate and help prosecute criminal complaints, and refer victims to other governmental and nongovernmental assistance agencies. Observers and assistance providers, however, reported that the NNP no longer operated these women's commissariats and instead had placed them and the investigation of these types of crimes with either regular police or the DAJ. Women's rights organizations claimed that NGOs or family members were barred from accompanying women when reporting domestic violence or sexual assaults and that the burden of gathering proof of the crime was often placed on the victim. Women's groups asserted the modest number of shelters (two government and 11 nongovernmental) was inadequate, especially on the Caribbean Coast, where only one shelter (nongovernmental) operated in the RACN.

Sexual Harassment: The law prohibits sexual harassment, and those convicted face one- to three-year sentences in prison, or three to five years if the victim is under 18 years old. Observers believed sexual harassment likely was underreported due to the failure of authorities to consider the abuse seriously and victims' fear of retribution.

Reproductive Rights: Couples and individuals have the right to decide the number, spacing, and timing of their children; manage their reproductive health; and have access to the information and means to do so, free from discrimination, coercion, or violence. The 2015 World Health Organization figures estimated the maternal mortality rate to be 150 deaths per 100,000 live births. Women in some areas, such as the RACN and the RACS, did not have widespread access to medical care or programs, and maternal death was more likely to affect poor rural women than their urban counterparts.

Emergency health care was generally provided, but in some cases women were afraid to seek medical treatment for post abortion obstetric emergencies, due to a "no exceptions" ban on abortion. Observers noted the Ministry of Health continued to make progress in quality, coverage, distribution, and usage of contraceptives through successful family planning programs.

Discrimination: The law provides for gender equality. Nevertheless, women often experienced discrimination in employment, credit, and pay equity for similar work, as well as in owning and managing businesses. Women were much less likely to be senior officials or managers. Authorities often discriminated in property matters against poor women who lacked birth certificates or identity cards. The Office of the Human Rights Ombudsman's special prosecutor for women and the Nicaraguan Women's Ministry, the government entities responsible for protecting women's rights, had limited effectiveness.

Children

Birth Registration: Citizenship is derived by birth within the country's territory and from one's parents. Local civil registries register births within 12 months; however, many persons, especially in rural areas, lacked birth certificates. Persons without citizenship documents were unable to obtain national identity cards and consequently had difficulty participating in the legal economy, conducting bank transactions, or voting. Such persons also were subject to restrictions in employment, access to courts, and land ownership.

The government continued to register newborns through service desks in public hospitals and through "social-promoter" programs that visited rural neighborhoods. MiFamilia, the Civil Registry, and, to a lesser extent, the CSE are responsible for registering births, but they did not make data available.

Child Abuse: The NNP reported that in 2015, the most recent period for which data was available, authorities received 889 complaints of sex crimes against adolescent girls. Human rights groups expressed concern over levels of child pregnancy throughout the country. High rates of sexual violence against teenage girls contributed to teenage pregnancy rates, according to Plan International.

Early and Forced Marriage: The minimum legal age for marriage is 18 years for men and women, or 16 with parental authorization. There were credible reports of forced early marriages in some rural indigenous communities. The UN Children's Fund's *2016 State of the World's Children* reported that 41 percent of women 20 to 24 years of age were married or in a union by age 18 and 10 percent were married by age 15. No information was available on government efforts to address or prevent forced and early marriage, and some advocates claimed the government did not enforce the law effectively.

Sexual Exploitation of Children: The Trafficking in Persons Law, which came into effect in 2015, prohibits sexual exploitation in general and designates enticing children or adolescents to engage in sexual activity as an aggravating condition. The government generally enforced the law when pertaining to child prostitution. Penalties include 10 to 15 years in prison for a person who entices or forces any individual to engage in sexual activity, and 19 to 20 years in prison for the same acts involving children or adolescents. The law defines statutory rape as sexual relations with children who are 14 or younger. Several NGOs reported sexual exploitation of young girls was common, as was the prevalence of older men (including foreigners) who exploited young girls under the guise of providing them support.

The law also prohibits child pornography, and the government generally enforced this law. The penalty for an individual convicted of inducing, facilitating, promoting, or using a minor for sexual or erotic purposes is 10 to 15 years in prison.

The country was a destination for child sex tourism. The law imposes a penalty of five to seven years in prison for convicted child-sex tourists. There were anecdotal reports of child-sex tourism in the Granada, Rivas, Chinandega, and Managua departments; there were no officially reported cases.

International Child Abductions: The country is a party to the 1980 Hague Convention on the Civil Aspects of International Child Abduction. See the Department of State's *Annual Report on International Parental Child Abduction* at travel.state.gov/content/childabduction/en/legal/compliance.html.

Anti-Semitism

According to the Nicaraguan Israelite Congregation, the recognized Jewish community in Nicaragua numbered approximately 50 members. There were no known reports of anti-Semitic acts.

Trafficking in Persons

See the Department of State's *Trafficking in Persons Report* at www.state.gov/j/tip/rls/tiprpt/.

Persons with Disabilities

The law prohibits discrimination against persons with physical, sensory, intellectual, and mental disabilities, but such discrimination was widespread in education, transportation, access to health care, the provision of state services, and employment. Laws related to persons with disabilities do not stipulate penalties for noncompliance, although penalties may be issued under the general labor inspection code. MiFamilia, the Ministry of Labor, and the PDDH are among government agencies responsible for the protection and advancement of rights of persons with disabilities. The government did not enforce the law effectively; did not mandate accessibility to buildings, information, and communications; and did not make information available on efforts to improve respect for the rights of persons with disabilities. Independent media reported that persons with disabilities accounted for less than 1 percent of public sector employees, despite the legally mandated minimum representation of 2 percent. Further reports indicated that public institutions did not sufficiently coordinate with the Labor Ministry to accommodate persons with disabilities in the workplace.

Persons with disabilities faced severe problems accessing schools, public health facilities, and other public institutions. Many voting facilities were not accessible to persons with disabilities. Complaints continued regarding the lack of accessible public transportation in Managua. While some buses were accessible, drivers of these buses reportedly either refused to stop to allow persons with disabilities to board or intentionally broke lift and ramp equipment. The press reported that the Managua Mayor's Office sponsored training for bus drivers through transportation cooperatives. The PDDH special prosecutor for disability rights was active throughout the year. Government clinics and hospitals provided care for veterans and other persons with disabilities, but the quality of care generally was poor.

National/Racial/Ethnic Minorities

Various indigenous and other ethnic groups from the RACN and the RACS attributed the lack of government resources devoted to the Caribbean Coast to discriminatory attitudes toward the ethnic and racial minorities in those regions. While the racial makeup of the RACN and the RACS historically has been Afro-descendent and Amerindian, increasing migration from the interior and Pacific Coast of the country made these groups a minority in many areas.

Exclusionary treatment based on race, skin color, and ethnicity was common, especially in higher-income urban areas. Darker-skinned persons of African descent from the RACN and the RACS, along with others assumed to be from those areas experienced discrimination, such as extra security measures and illegal searches by police.

Indigenous People

Indigenous people constituted approximately 5 percent of the population and lived primarily in the RACN and the RACS. They often did not participate in decisions affecting their lands, cultures, and traditions or the exploitation of energy, minerals, timber, and other natural resources on their lands. Individuals from five major indigenous groups--the Miskito, Sumo/Mayangna, Garifuna (of Afro-Amerindian origin), Creole, and Rama--alleged government discrimination through underrepresentation in the legislative branch.

Indigenous people from rural areas often lacked birth certificates, identity cards, and land titles. Although they formed political groups, these often held little influence and were ignored or used by major national parties to advance the latter's own agendas. Most indigenous people in rural areas lacked access to public services, and deteriorating roads made medicine and health care almost unobtainable for many. The rates of unemployment, illiteracy, and truancy were among the highest in the country. Some indigenous groups continued to lack educational materials in their native languages and relied on Spanish-language texts provided by the national government.

NGOs and indigenous rights groups claimed the government failed to protect the civil and political rights of indigenous communities. Some observers alleged government involvement in the violence against Miskito populations in the RACN along the Coco River, either as a result of inaction or more directly as accomplices to nonindigenous groups invading indigenous lands. According to media reports and local indigenous groups, violence resulted in as many as 40 deaths between 2015 and the first nine months of 2016, including two beheadings, and accounted for the displacement of as many as 1,000 persons into neighboring towns, such as Bilwi, and across the border into Honduras. The IACHR issued three separate precautionary measures in response to the violence. The government largely ignored the issuances but answered one precautionary measure in a public letter; however, it failed to address potential solutions.

Indigenous women faced multiple levels of discrimination based on their ethnicity, gender, and lower economic status.

The National Commission of Demarcation and Titling, Attorney General's Office, and Nicaraguan Institute of Territorial Studies did not make any progress in demarcating indigenous lands. Additionally, the government failed to relocate or remove nonindigenous populations from ancestral indigenous lands, leading to significant violence throughout the year, specifically in the RACN.

Representatives of autonomous regions and indigenous communities regularly noted the government failed to invest in infrastructure. Throughout the year indigenous leaders alleged regional and national governments granted logging concessions to private firms and government-affiliated businesses, such as ALBA-Forestal, and logging continued in violation of national autonomy laws in the RACS and the RACN.

Indigenous groups were increasingly concerned about violations of their rights in connection with plans to build an interoceanic canal. Many allege that the concession to do so was granted illegally and without the required consultations with the indigenous community. For example, while the president of the Rama-Creole government had signed an authorization for the canal to be built on Rama-Creole land, members of the indigenous territorial government had not consented to his doing so. Indigenous groups, moreover, are not members of the Grand Canal Authority, which oversees the implementation of the canal project and was also established without consultations. There were a limited number of presentations on the canal to indigenous populations, but groups claim these were inadequate.

Violations of indigenous lands continued in the Bosawas Biosphere Reserve, RACN, according to press reports. The Mayangna indigenous group, which has territorial rights to much of the Bosawas Reserve, strongly criticized the government's unwillingness to prevent alleged land grabs by nonindigenous settlers, as well as illegal logging and other exploitation of natural resources. This also occurred regularly in the Indio Maiz Reserve.

Acts of Violence, Discrimination, and Other Abuses Based on Sexual Orientation and Gender Identity

Although sexual orientation is not mentioned specifically, the law states all persons are equal before the law and provides for the right to equal protection. LGBTI persons, however, continued to face widespread societal discrimination and abuse, particularly in housing, education, and employment. The LGBTI community generally believed the special prosecutor for sexual diversity had insufficient resources. No specific laws exist to punish hate crimes against LGBTI groups. The family code, a set of laws pertaining to family-related matters, establishes that a family comprises a man and a woman joined in marriage or common-law marriage. This discriminatory definition most affected the LGBTI community in the areas of adoption and access to social security benefits.

HIV and AIDS Social Stigma

The law provides specific protections for persons with HIV/AIDS against discrimination in employment and health services, but such persons continued to suffer societal discrimination. Although some improvements were recognized among health-care workers after training, a lack of awareness and education persisted in that sector and in the public generally regarding the prevention, treatment, and transmission of HIV/AIDS.

A nondiscrimination administrative resolution issued by the Ministry of Health establishes methods to file complaints against health workers in cases of discrimination against persons working in prostitution, HIV/AIDS patients, or on the basis of gender orientation. The resolution also establishes sanctions for health workers found to have discriminated against patients for these reasons.

Section 7. Worker Rights

a. Freedom of Association and the Right to Collective Bargaining

The law provides for the right of all workers in the public and private sectors, with the exception of those in the military and police, to form and join independent unions of their choice without prior authorization and to bargain collectively. The constitution recognizes the right to strike, although it places some restrictions on this right. The law prohibits antiunion discrimination and requires reinstatement of workers fired for union activity. Nevertheless, employers routinely used their right to obtain the Ministry of Labor's permission to dismiss any employee, including union organizers, immediately after being reinstated, provided the employer agrees to pay double the usual severance pay. Burdensome and lengthy conciliation procedures impeded workers' ability to call strikes. Additionally, if a strike continues for 30 days without resolution, the Ministry of Labor has authority to suspend the strike and submit the matter to arbitration.

A collective bargaining agreement cannot exceed two years and is renewed automatically if neither party requests its revision. Companies in disputes with their employees must negotiate with the employees' union, if one exists. By law several unions may coexist at any one enterprise, and the law permits management to sign separate collective bargaining agreements with each union.

With some exceptions, the government effectively enforced applicable laws and often sought to foster resolution of labor conflicts through informal negotiations rather than formal administrative or judicial processes. The law does not establish specific fines, and observers claimed penalties were generally insufficient to deter violations. Although the law establishes a labor court arbitration process, it was subject to long wait times and lengthy and complicated procedures, and many labor disputes were resolved out of court. The Labor Ministry claimed it oversaw 19,651 labor disputes in 2014, the last year for which information was publicly available. Of these disputes, 7,148 were dealt with through an agreement, and 12,503 were dealt with in court. Labor and human rights organizations continued to allege rulings were often unfavorable to workers. Representatives of a foreign firm alleged that a Ministry of Labor official prohibited them from permanently closing their factory, laying off their employees, and leaving the country ahead of the November 6 presidential election.

Freedom of association and the right to collective bargaining were generally respected, but, as in other cases involving independent groups, the government often intervened for political reasons. Most labor unions were allied with political parties, and in recent years the government reportedly illegally dissolved unions and fired workers not associated with the ruling FSLN. Independent organizations, however, were no longer keeping track of the severity of the situation. Former ministry employees and human rights and labor organizations alleged pro-FSLN public sector unions used intimidation and coercion to recruit new members, often pressuring workers to leave non-FSLN unions.

Politically motivated firings of workers continued to be a problem. Observers noted that the firings were carried out for political reasons, such as refusal of the worker to join the FSLN or participate in FSLN demonstrations. Moreover, party affiliation or a letter of recommendation from party secretaries, family cabinet coordinators or other party officials was allegedly required from applicants seeking a public sector job. Several sources argued similar instances of public sector employees being fired without receiving severance pay continued to occur.

There were no known high-profile documented instances of strikes being declared illegal. During a strike, employers cannot hire replacement workers, but unions alleged this practice was common. Wildcat strikes--those without union authorization--have historically been common.

Employers interfered in the functioning of workers' organizations and committed other violations related to freedom of association and collective bargaining. Labor leaders noted employers routinely violated collective bargaining agreements and labor laws with impunity.

Many employers in the formal sector continued to blacklist or fire union members and did not reinstate them. Many of these cases did not reach the court system or a mediation process led by the Ministry of Labor. Employers often delayed severance payments to fired workers or omitted the payments altogether. Employers also avoided legal penalties by organizing employer-led unions that lacked independence and frequently using contract workers to replace striking employees. There were reports party dues were automatically deducted from paychecks.

b. Prohibition of Forced or Compulsory Labor

The law prohibits all forms of forced or compulsory labor. Penalties for violations range from 10 to 20 years in prison but were generally insufficient to deter violations. There was no information available regarding government enforcement of these laws. Despite reported political will to combat human trafficking, including labor trafficking, during the year the government prosecuted and convicted fewer traffickers than in the previous year and provided only limited information about its law enforcement efforts.

Observers noted reports of forced labor, including of men, women, and children subjected to forced labor in agriculture and domestic servitude.

Also see the Department of State's *Trafficking in Persons Report* at www.state.gov/j/tip/rls/tiprpt/.

c. Prohibition of Child Labor and Minimum Age for Employment

The law establishes the minimum age for employment at 14 and limits the workday for any individual between ages 14 and 18 to six hours and the workweek to 30 hours. Those between 14 and 16 must have parental approval to work or enter into a formal labor contract. The law prohibits teenage domestic workers from sleeping in the houses of their employers. It is illegal for minors to work in places the Ministry of Labor considers harmful to their health or safety, such as mines, garbage dumps, and night entertainment venues, and to undertake certain agricultural work. The law provides for eight-year prison terms and substantial fines for persons employing children in dangerous work and permits inspectors to close those facilities.

The government used its limited resources to concentrate on child labor violations in select sectors in narrow geographic areas, such as coffee growing regions, and gave only limited attention to the large informal sector.

The government continued Programa Amor, which aimed to eradicate child labor by reintegrating abandoned children into society. Information on the program's activities, funding, and effectiveness was unavailable.

Child labor remained widespread. A 2005 National Institute of Development Information national survey of adolescent and child labor (the most recent statistics available) estimated there were 238,800 working children between five and 17 years old, of whom 80 percent performed high-risk labor and 36 percent were younger than 14. According to organizations that worked on children's rights, this likely increased to almost 320,000 children working in some form of child labor. A common feature of child labor was the prevalence of unpaid family work, and the institute stated 80 percent of children and adolescents were unpaid workers.

Most child labor occurred in forestry, fishing, and the informal sector, including on coffee plantations and subsistence farms. Child labor also occurred in the production of dairy products, oranges, bananas, tobacco, palm products, coffee, rice, and sugarcane; cattle raising; street sales; garbage-dump scavenging; stone crushing; street performing; and transport.

Children working in agriculture suffered from sun exposure, extreme temperatures, and dangerous pesticides and other chemicals. Children working in the fishing industry were at risk from polluted water and dangerous ocean conditions.

Also see the Department of Labor's *Findings on the Worst Forms of Child Labor* at www.dol.gov/ilab/reports/child-labor/findings/.

d. Discrimination with Respect to Employment and Occupation

Labor laws and regulations prohibit discrimination regarding race, sex, gender, disability, language, sexual orientation and/or gender identity, HIV or other communicable disease status, or social status. The government did not effectively enforce these laws and regulations.

Discrimination in employment and occupation occurred with respect to women, persons with disabilities, sexual orientation, and gender identity (see section 6).

e. Acceptable Conditions of Work

The law establishes a statutory minimum wage for 10 economic sectors. It is calculated differently for each sector, and the average was 5,151 cordobas ($180) per month. According to the Ministry of Labor, the average legal minimum wage covers 35 percent of the cost of basic goods.

In general, the minimum wage was enforced only in the formal sector, estimated to be approximately 20 percent of the economy. The Ministry of Labor is the primary enforcement agency, but the government did not allocate adequate staff or resources to enable the Office of Hygiene and Occupational Safety to enforce occupational safety and health provisions. Established penalties were generally sufficient to deter violations.

The standard legal workweek is a maximum of 48 hours, with one day of rest. The law dictates an obligatory year-end bonus equivalent to one month's pay, proportional to the number of months worked. The law mandates premium pay for overtime, prohibits compulsory overtime, and sets a maximum of three hours of overtime per day not to exceed nine hours per week. The law establishes occupational health and safety standards. Such standards were not current or appropriate for the main production activities in the country.

The National Council of Labor Hygiene and Safety, including its departmental committees, is responsible for implementing worker safety legislation and collaborating with other government agencies and civil society organizations in developing assistance programs and promoting training and prevention activities. According to the Ministry of Labor's 2014 annual report, it carried out 1,382 labor hygiene and safety inspections, leading to 14 fines.

Health and safety standards were not widely enforced in the large informal sector, which represents 77 percent of employment and 90 percent of businesses. The informal sector included the bulk of workers in street sales, agriculture and ranching, transportation, domestic labor, fishing, and minor construction. Legal limitations on hours worked often were ignored by employers, who claimed workers readily volunteered for extra hours for additional pay. Violations of wage and hour regulations in the informal sector were common and generally not investigated, particularly in street sales, domestic work, and agriculture. Compulsory overtime was reported in the private security sector, where guards often were required to work excessive shifts without relief.

By law workers can remove themselves from situations that endanger their health or safety without jeopardy to their employment. It was unclear if authorities effectively protected employees in all such cases.